I0814544

# THE POCKET DREAM READER

Published in 2025
by Gemini Books
Part of Gemini Books Group

Based in Woodbridge and London

Marine House, Tide Mill Way
Woodbridge, Suffolk IP12 1AP
United Kingdom

www.geminibooks.com


Part of the Gemini Pockets series

Cover image: Shutterstock/MR SOCCER

ISBN 978-1-80247-282-0



A CIP catalogue record for this book is available from the British Library.

Manufacturer's EU Representative: Eurolink Compliance Limited, 25 Herbert Place, Dublin, D02 AY86, Republic of Ireland. admin@eurolink-europe.ie.



Printed in China

10 9 8 7 6 5 4 3 2 1

**Images**: Shutterstock: 4, 5 / johnpluto; 6 / Serghei Starus; 28 / titoOnz; 46 / Triff; 66 / IgorZh; 86 / andreiuc88; 108 / Volha Vasilevich. Freepik: Background cloud texture.

# THE POCKET

Interpret the symbols, signs & meanings

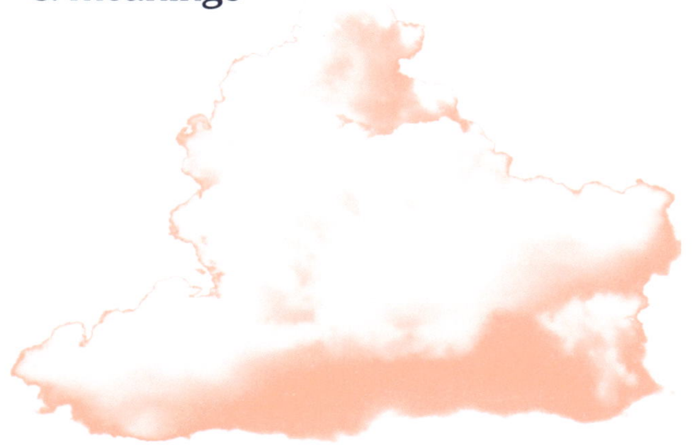

# DREAM READER

# CONTENTS

# Introduction

We have been fascinated by dreams since ancient times, believing they offer a door to our subconscious, unlocking mysteries and showing ways forward in our everyday lives.

Many cultures and belief systems offer methods to interpret our dreams. In the early 20th century, psychologists Sigmund Freud and Carl Jung famously explored their own interpretations of these psychic treasure troves. Today, dream analysis blends historic and modern elements, including a wide range of spiritual and cultural perspectives, to propel personal growth.

Read on to explore the captivating world of dreams. Decode their symbols and hidden meanings to better understand your waking life.

Be curious. Be open. And be ready to receive amazing insights from your subconscious self.

# Keep a dream diary

Analyzing your dreams is a deeply personal and unique process. There are some common approaches to help you get started and it becomes easier with practice.

The first step to interpreting your dreams is to keep a dream diary. Dream researchers recommend writing down dreams immediately on waking. This will help you recall details and analyze their content.

Keeping a dream diary will also help you notice any patterns emerging and relate your dreams to your life experience.

# Dream diary tips

- Keep a notebook and pen beside your bed, and record your dreams immediately upon waking.

- If you wake during the night, write down or voice-memo the main themes of the dream or one or two key elements. The rest of it will come to you in the morning, with help from these brief prompts.

- Try to write down a snapshot of the feelings and emotions that accompanied the dream.

- You will find spontaneous dream recall increases as you practise this discipline.

# Interpreting your dreams

Dreams are emblematic: they reflect you at a core level. Using your dream diary, look for elements in each dream to explore. These might be people, actions, events, colours or feelings.

The signs and symbols that appear are not by chance – they are personal and will carry specific meanings for you. Explore their context within the dream. For example, is the dream centred on a particular person, or does an item appear on the peripheries, just noticeable?

While it's often helpful to recall a dream in conversation with a loved one, remember that the best person to analyze a dream is the dreamer.

# How to interpret your dreams

- Always try to interpret your dream the morning after having it – this is when you will get the most out of the themes and symbols included.
- Remember, dreams contain symbolic messages – look beyond the obvious.
- Look for recurring themes or patterns. These may reflect a current life issue or emotional state.
- Examine real-life connections – there may be an event that is bringing up unresolved feelings, or a person who makes you feel a certain way.
- Consider what unconscious fears or desires may be underlying the events in your dreams. Use this as an opportunity not only for self-discovery but also personal growth.
- Decoding dreams is a subjective process: trust your instincts but try to also be open to multiple interpretations.

**“The interpretation of dreams is the royal road to a knowledge of the unconscious activities of the mind.”**

Sigmund Freud,
*The Interpretation of Dreams* (1900)

# Freud & dream interpretation

Recognized as the father of psychoanalysis, Sigmund Freud wrote in *The Interpretation of Dreams*, published in 1900, that interpreting dreams is "the royal road" to understanding our unconscious mind.

One of the most important books of the 20th century, it was his first significant attempt to expound his theory of a dynamic unconscious, created during our childhood and active throughout our lives.

Everyone dreams. And these dreams, Freud understood, are a window into our most powerful desires, our greatest fears and our fiercest internal conflicts – all largely hidden from our conscious awareness.

Through psychoanalysis, Freud sought to interpret dreams to reveal the profound role played by our unconscious mind in our conscious lives.

# The 5 most common dreams

1 Falling (page 32)

2 Flying (page 34)

3 Being chased (page 52)

4 Losing teeth (page 44)

5 Being naked in public (page 38)

**“Dreams often surprise us into the strangest self-knowledge... Dreaming is the truest confessional.”**

Alexander Smith,
*On Dreams and Dreaming* (1914)

# Jung on dreams

Psychologist and psychiatrist Carl Jung did not see dreams as random emanations of our unconscious mind, but as spontaneous messages, prompted by our psyche's efforts to be whole.

He believed that dreams are symbolic, and can have many different meanings, so must be considered with an open mind. He taught that dreams should be explored in order to bring resolution to hidden emotional issues. He also warned that engaging with the unconscious may bring up things you don't want to face.

Each dream symbol meaning is unique to you, though there are some archetypal motifs, like a mother figure. Although a coherent message from your unconscious, your dream is cloaked in symbolism and should not be interpreted literally.

**“Dreams are the facts from which we must proceed.”**

Carl Jung,
*Memories, Dreams, Reflections* (1961)

**“I often think of dreaming as simply thinking in a different biochemical state.”**

Deirdre Barrett,
Harvard psychologist,
*TIME* (12 September 2017)

# Theories of dreaming

Contemporary researchers are wary of Freudian ideas that dreams are meaningful, and also of the Jungian belief that dreams can heal unresolved emotional issues.

The modern understanding of dreams often draws on groundbreaking neuroscientific studies. Some psychologists hypothesize dreams:

- Help to regulate emotions by creating memories of them.
- Are simply the brain trying to interpret cortical activity or external stimuli while we sleep.
- Keep the brain active to help it function well.
- Result from the "pruning" of neural connections, the clearing of clutter.

# Nightmares

A nightmare is a type of dream that is often upsetting, unsettling, distressing and quite vivid.

Known to wake a dreamer from sleep, often in fear, many therapists and scientists believe nightmares are revealing anxieties we have avoided or buried.

There can be many reasons for nightmares: you may be going through a time of stress or change, or you may have some anxiety regarding a loved one. Common nightmares include:

- Being unable to find a toilet - you may still be learning to express your needs.

- A car crash - perhaps you are not feeling in control of your life choices or path.

- Being lost - you are looking for guidance or wanting change.

If you are grieving, taking medication or experiencing mental health issues, nightmares can become more frequent.

# Interpreting nightmares

It might not feel like it at the time, but nightmares can actually be beneficial. They can often point to things you may be missing in your daily life. They can also give insights into your emotional state, or offer a chance to look at any trauma or major life issues in a more symbolic way.

- Use your nightmares as a chance to really look at any unresolved anxieties or traumas you are not dealing with in your waking life.

- Nightmares can provoke such a strong emotional reaction that they can be a positive catalyst for change, helping you find ways through uncertainty or worry.

- Take note that nightmares, while upsetting in the moment, are more of a tool to help you resolve issues. You are in control of how you perceive them.

# Lucid dreaming

Do you ever become fully aware you are dreaming, even though you are technically still asleep?

If so, you have experienced a lucid dream! In this state, you can exercise a degree of control over your dream, even directing it down a certain path or leading yourself to powerful insights.

It may be possible to train yourself to have more lucid dreams (they are relatively rare, with only 5 per cent of us experiencing them regularly).

Research suggests that lucid dreaming takes place during the REM (rapid eye movement) stage of the sleep cycle (entered into approximately every five hours).

Some people set alarms to wake them during the night, so they can again enter REM.

When you are ready to sleep, visualize what you want to dream about, detailing places and events as specifically as possible in your mind. Repeat a phrase such as: "When I dream I will remember I am dreaming" to yourself as you drift off.

# False awakening

This is a dream event where you believe you are awake, but you are dreaming!

These dreams tend to occur during the REM phase of sleep, sometimes multiple times in a row, and can be extraordinarily vivid and realistic.

Common dreamed experiences can be quite basic, including tasks such as getting ready for the day, visiting the toilet or even simply walking into the kitchen.

Because they can be so true to life, it can be confusing and disorientating upon waking. Take your time!

**“The dream is the small hidden door in the deepest and most intimate sanctum of the soul, which opens to that primeval cosmic night that was soul long before there was conscious ego and will be soul far beyond what a conscious ego could ever reach.”**

Carl Jung,
*The Meaning of Psychology for Modern Man* (1931)

# Recurring dreams

Nearly three quarters of us have recurring dreams. When we experience the same dream on repeat (more than once a night, or over a few days or weeks), this may result from challenging issues or emotional turmoil. Our subconscious may be repeating the same themes to compel us to try to resolve a problem.

Common recurring dreams include falling (linked to a feeling of loss of control); being chased (feeling overwhelmed); and our teeth falling out (believed to signal anxiety).

To stop recurring dreams, try to resolve what is worrying you emotionally and develop healthy bedtime routines: go to bed at a regular time and avoid caffeine, alcohol, nicotine and using digital devices before sleep.

# Daydreaming

Studies show we spend up to 50 per cent of our waking hours daydreaming!

But what is it? Some believe it is a refocusing of attention from the external world to our inner world, a place where your mind can wander through your thoughts and feelings at its own leisure.

Neuroscientists have suggested that daydreaming or mind wandering is a normal resting state of our brains, and one that is needed for us to be ready to fire on all cylinders. Research shows that daydreaming can reduce stress and enhance creativity.

Some of the most common themes in daydreams are: adventure, heroism, power, romance, metamorphosis, fame, animals and food.

**“Truth and dreams are twins.”**

Austin O’Malley,
*Keystones of Thought* (1914)

# Chapter One

## YOUR BODY

Dying

Falling

Flying

Being unable to move

Being naked in public

Being pregnant

Being unable to speak

Losing teeth

# Dying

While dreaming of death can be very scary, it often does not link specifically to dying at all.

Instead, a death dream is often representative of change, the end of a chapter, or an end of life as you know it.

While such dreams often symbolize a major life transition such as a relationship breakup, relocating or leaving a job, it can also announce inner changes, transformation and self-discovery.

Dreams about others dying can also symbolize changes in a relationship or worries about someone's physical health. If they involve killing someone, it can relate to a toxic relationship or unhealthy circumstance – like a job that you aren't happy in.

## Interpretations

- A current struggle with grief.
- Feeling unsafe.
- A natural death represents an organic change that has or is taking place.
- A murder can symbolize a change that is forced upon you.
- The person who dies can represent a characteristic of the dreamer.
- Dreams of animals dying are associated with anticipatory grief.
- Dreaming of suicide can be very scary, but the meaning of this dream is actually positive, representing the shedding of something old.

## Opportunities for growth

- Focus on self-care and on improving your mental health.
- Find ways to manage stress – including taking regular exercise and a daily stretching routine.

# Falling

Most people have experienced the sensation of falling in a dream. It is one of the most realistic feelings while asleep!

Falling from the sky is a central and repeating motif, which is associated with feelings of anxiety or even betrayal.

There are also variations on this theme, such as falling through the floor, which relate to fear that may arise from sudden changes such as losing a job.

Falling dreams are particularly common for those suffering from PTSD, so ensure you are also being supported by a doctor.

## Interpretations

- This dream asks, "What can you accept about yourself versus what parts do you most want to hide from?"
- There is an aspect of the self that is falling away.
- Feeling overwhelmed after some kind of failure or falling from grace – a loss of reputation.
- A feeling of losing a grip on a situation or feeling out of control.

## Opportunities for growth

- Find ways to support yourself when you are feeling overwhelmed or anxious.
- Speak to friends and family or find a support group where you can share your worries and feel listened to in a non-judgemental way.

# Flying

Dreams about flying can offer a liberating and exhilarating experience, accompanied by a feeling of being completely free.

Associated with notions of rising above a challenging situation, such dreams can also be related to navigating your own way in life, or can reflect a yearning for more independence, freedom or empowerment.

## Interpretations

- This dream asks, "What is holding you down?"
- Reveals yearnings for change or longings for an escape from a current situation.
- Expresses the need for exploration or the pursuit of new creative ideas.
- Explores ideas of mastery and a belief that nothing is impossible.
- Expresses longings for freedom from gravity and worldly limitations.

## Opportunities for growth

- This dream is a reminder of the higher states we can experience, free from our worries and anxieties.
- This is a special and uplifting dream – use its positive message to infuse your waking life.

# Being unable to move

Dreams where you are unable to move your body are common, but this does not make them less vivid or frightening.

Dreams may involve you being trapped in an enclosed space or being restrained or paralyzed.

Most often, this dream is taken to symbolize psychological distress and anxiety that may stem from current life events: perhaps there are some big upheavals that are occurring or there is frustration about some level of indecision.

## Interpretations

- Opposing ideas are colliding within your psyche.
- You are waiting for important test results.
- You are working in a job that no longer feeds your soul.
- You are experiencing relationship issues that are creating triggers.
- There may be situations where you are dependent on another person or event to occur before your situation will resolve itself.

## Opportunities for growth

- Focus on self-care and on improving your mental health.
- Find ways to manage stress – including taking regular exercise and a daily stretching routine.

# Being naked in public

You are in a crowded public place, you look down... and you realize you are not wearing anything. At all. Not even a hat. No socks. No underwear. Nada.

This jarring experience makes you feel panicked, defenceless and embarrassed, but it is a perfectly normal dream with universal themes.

There may be feelings of vulnerability, fears of exposure or even anxieties about being judged. Such a dream really questions what you are hiding from!

## Interpretations

- This dream asks, "What can you accept about yourself versus what parts do you most want to hide from?"
- There is an insecurity around being watched closely.
- There could be strong feelings around body image.
- Imposter syndrome is present.
- Expresses the fear that there are parts of you that you believe others will find unacceptable.

## Opportunities for growth

- Use the self-awareness gained from this dream to nurture a more authentic relationship with the world.
- Build your sense of identity from within, and not based on other people's opinions.
- If you feel the dream may be pointing to negative views of your own body, focus on where you find your self-worth.

# Being pregnant

You may dream that you yourself are pregnant, or that someone close to you is. Often in this dream you are very far along in your pregnancy, cradling a full bump, which makes the sensation of this dream even more shocking.

While dreaming of pregnancy can be interpreted as a desire to start a family, it also has symbolic significance in birthing new ideas or creative projects, and a desire for fresh opportunities.

This could be a sign that change is on the horizon and that you are ready to welcome new beginnings.

It is not only women that experience this dream – it's also common for men to dream of having a baby bump!

## Interpretations

- There may be literal interpretations of this dream, related to parenthood.
- This could represent a very deep desire to have children, or you could be concerned about your ability as a parent.
- Anxiety around a pregnancy could mean you are anxious about events outside your control.
- Pregnancy also signifies change, new life and a desire for something to come to fruition.

## Opportunities for growth

- This dream can help you focus on personal growth, hope and creativity.
- It can turn your attention to any parts of your life that need nurturing or caring for.
- Take this as a sign to open yourself up to new possibilities.

# Being unable to speak

Dreams where you are unable to speak can have a direct correlation with the feeling of not being heard in your day-to-day life.

It may point toward inner conflict and issues of low self-esteem. Emotions that accompany this dream include frustration, anger and helplessness.

There may be issues around self-assertiveness, self-confidence and self-expression that need exploring.

## Interpretations

- This dream asks, “What emotional barriers are stopping you from expressing yourself?”
- Expresses frustration and psychological distress around communication.
- Shows feelings of being repressed or lacking control.
- Conveys a sense of being unheard or misunderstood, tongue-tied, underappreciated or unvalued.
- Can represent being blocked creatively.

## Opportunities for growth

- Examine psychological blockages to clear communication and learn to express your needs and stand up for yourself.
- Consider if pride or self-sabotage stop you from telling others what you want.

# Losing teeth

Apparently, around 40 per cent of us dream about our teeth falling out!

This rather disturbing subject has connotations of loss: perhaps of a job, a relationship or the physical passing of a family member.

It is also seen to herald a major transition, such as from childhood to adulthood, where teeth are lost and replaced anew.

## Interpretations

- Can be associated with lengthy periods of anxiety.
- An expression of acute periods of uncontrolled stress or longer-term depression.
- In some cases, relating to jealousy or a health-related fear.
- Can symbolize something necessary and important being taken away, or moving from one time of your life into another.

## Opportunities for growth

- Be aware of the need to spend more time nurturing your inner self.
- Focus on acceptance – this could help if you are experiencing life upheavals or unwanted change.

# Chapter Two

## DREAMING EXPERIENCES

The apocalypse
Being arrested
Being chased
Driving
Fireworks
Running late
Spying
Taking a test
Winning the lottery

# The apocalypse

You are suddenly confronted by a momentous event that is out of your control and with life-altering consequences.

This is the ultimate symbol of change.

Perhaps the dream involves the main sources of power in your life – whether a spouse or a parent – or it might have work connotations.

Whatever the setting, it is an unsettling and threatening dream with traumatic impact.

## Interpretations

- An apocalyptic dream on the theme of water relates to unresolved emotions.
- Themes about global destruction are driven by hyper-anxious emotions or issues to do with finances.
- Possibly a metaphor for a life-changing finale, such as how a teenager may feel about their parents' divorce.
- Anxieties about the state of the world generally.

## Opportunities for growth

- The opportunity for self-reflection can herald a spiritual awakening.
- Direct your attention toward a transformation of your identity and sense of self.
- Focus on self-care the day after a dream of this nature.

# Being arrested

Dreams about being arrested make an uncomfortable topic, with dramatic effect.

Perhaps it is an expression of intense feelings that may be present about a life situation; they may even express a more literal reflection of guilt and remorse.

Alternatively, such drama may reflect feelings of injustice and unfairness that you harbour about your life.

## Interpretations

- Could indicate that you may be taking a lot of risks.
- There may be a feeling of being boxed in, or that no-one is paying attention to your dissatisfaction.
- If handcuffed, this indicates a situation where someone (possibly you) is being particularly controlled.
- If you are arresting someone else, it can mean you are being too controlling and it is not productive.

## Opportunities for growth

- You need to be more assertive around your rights.
- Consider the balance of power in your life – are there areas of control you need to release, or boundaries that need to be established?

# Being chased

Dreams about being chased are one of the most common across cultures and over the centuries. Perhaps more of a nightmare than a dream, it is reassuring to know that it does not need to be taken literally.

Such dreams can mean there is something you are not facing up to in your life, whether it is a coming deadline, a health concern or financial issue.

For a positive interpretation, if you are the chaser in the dream, rather than being chased, this reflects that you may be attracting a partner or overtaking a competitor in your life.

## Interpretations

- Running from a wild animal is often interpreted as a suppression of love or sexuality.
- Being chased by a monster that will harm you suggests there is a problem that will grow if it is not confronted.
- A high-speed boat or swim chase over water can be an expression of some overwhelming emotional states.

## Opportunities for growth

- Take note of who or what you are running from in your dream, and use it to try and identify the source of your apprehensive feelings.
- Use this dream to help you ask the question, "How can I face a current issue in a healthy way?"

# Driving

Dreams about driving are very revealing and a direct reflection of how we feel about our sense of direction in life. It can relate to the goals we set ourselves, and is also a symbol that relates to issues of independence and control.

Driving in the daytime represents a clear vision, while driving at night can symbolize how we are leaving the darkness behind us.

A crazy, out-of-control car trip reflects feelings of being overwhelmed, or that life is moving too fast to process.

## Interpretations

- If you are in the driving seat in your dream, it can indicate feelings of control and confidence.
- If you are a passenger and unhappy with the driver, someone else may be making decisions in your life that you feel you should be making yourself.
- If you have arrived safely at your destination, this suggests you are keeping your life on track.
- Slamming on the brakes suggests you may be reconsidering your current choices and are in the process of thinking things through.

## Opportunities for growth

- Use dreams about driving to be aware of which issues are occupying you at the moment.
- Use the context of this dream to review how you are progressing with certain decisions or in your life generally. Do you need to change course?

# Fireworks

These awe-inspiring displays from the subconscious carry messages of good fortune, spectacular achievements and the triumph of light over darkness.

Depending on whether you are the one setting them off, or simply watching – alone or in a crowd or with others – this dazzling, explosive dream can touch on themes of creativity, showing off, passion, love, romance and celebration.

## Interpretations

- Having this rare event occur in your dream can indicate a desire for attention and recognition.
- If you are the one lighting the fireworks, it may reveal a strong wish to express yourself.
- A large display with a crowd could signify that you are anticipating or seeking a grand celebration.
- Dream fireworks often mark changes for the better as well as reaching significant milestones.
- Fireworks denote a period of transformation, offering bursts of insight.

## Opportunities for growth

- Review how to overcome a problem or get through a big change to your circumstances.
- Harness the energy of this dream to help release any repressed feelings you have been harbouring.

# Running late

Dreams about running late often relate to an anxiety about something in the waking world. Usually, it is important that you are there for whatever you happen to be late for, and it's clear that you are not going to make it, though you continue to try.

These anxieties tend to revolve around expectations, goals or success levels. They can also represent missed opportunities, or possibilities that feel like they may be slipping away.

## Interpretations

- If you are late for a wedding, job interview, meeting or a date, this timeline-related anxiety dream can reveal a self-imposed pressure to succeed in a life-changing moment.
- If you are late for some form of travel (for example, bus, train, boat, aeroplane, taxi or metro), you could feel you are about to miss an opportunity.

## Opportunities for growth

- Dreams about being late could spur you on to review your life goals or work-based relationships and seek ways forward.
- You may want to take the chance on an opportunity you've had recently.
- Use this dream to reflect on any inabilities to meet expectations.

# Spying

Spy dreams are often associated with feelings of danger, exhilaration, apprehension, excitement, empowerment and intrigue.

You may have a fear of being deceived or manipulated, or harbour a desire for control and influence. Having a spy dream can also denote a sharpness of mind and the ability to see what others are missing – it could also point to skills in navigating complex situations.

Spying in a dream is sometimes symbolized by mind games, hidden agendas or a loss of privacy.

## Interpretations

- If you are being spied upon in your dream, you may be concealing sensitive emotions or secretive behaviours.
- If you are under constant surveillance in your dream, look for sources of mistrust in relationships.
- To be caught by a spy in your dream may mean that someone is trying to influence you or take advantage.
- If spies are harassing you, it indicates uneasiness and risky disputes, or the possibility that someone is gaining unfair insight.

## Opportunities for growth

- If you have a dream about being spied upon or being caught by a spy, ask yourself if you are experiencing trust issues, and seek a way to resolve this.
- Use this dream to spur you on through any complexities that are pressing in.

# Taking a test

Taking a test in a dream often reflects a common theme of being unprepared, or not expecting an exam. Unsurprisingly, it is often interpreted as being stress-related.

But dreaming of taking a test, or being tested, can also reflect a period of learning. It can even literally mean there is a part of you thinking of going back to school and starting a fresh career.

Sometimes this dream can be even more symbolic, representing feelings of uncertainty about how you might cope with a new challenge, such as parenthood.

## Interpretations

- Dreaming of taking a test can relate to a feeling of being tested by current or future circumstances.
- If you are dreaming of being late for a test, the message may be that you are sabotaging yourself.
- If you wake from this dream feeling anxious and wound up, you may be feeling unprepared for the moment you face in life.

## Opportunities for growth

- Having this dream can be indication to be gentle with yourself as life is a learning experience.
- Use this dream to ask yourself whether your beliefs and ways of thinking are still serving you, or whether they are worth examining afresh.

# Winning the lottery

This is an auspicious dream! It holds ideas of progress, growth, good luck, abundance and positive changes.

It can also symbolize gratitude for the blessings you have, or signify a period of abundance. Lottery wins in dreams may represent gaining recognition, respect, popularity, friendship and goodwill.

## Interpretations

- Dreams of winning the lottery are more closely linked to happiness and optimism than to finances.
- If you have this dream, you may be seeking ways of solving complex issues.
- These dreams could indicate a risk-taking aspect or reflect anxieties about finance.
- This dream can symbolize a strong sense of self-worth and an openness to receive.

## Opportunities for growth

- This optimistic dream can inspire you to forge positive developments in your relationship or work life.
- Use this dream to work on being more hopeful and on the lookout for the best in things

# Chapter Three

## RELATIONSHIPS & OTHERS

Abandonment

Baptism

Celebrities

Children

Choir

Divorce or relationship disharmony

Engagement

Infidelity

Deceased loved ones

# Abandonment

Familiar themes in abandonment dreams include anxiety, lack of control of your own life, difficulty in planning for the future and childhood traumas.

These types of dreams can be emotionally charged, and include feelings of loss, rejection or neglect. Abandonment can appear in myriad dream scenarios, but will usually involve exploring fears, insecurities and unresolved emotions.

To move forward, it can work best if you relate the specific emotions and symbols of the dream to your particular experience and relationships.

## Interpretations

- If you are abandoned by a spouse, this reflects anxieties within the relationship.
- If you are abandoned by family, it can relate to foundational fears about safety and stability.
- If you are being abandoned and betrayed, this generally relates to trust issues and fears around vulnerability.

## Opportunities for growth

- If you are the person being left, use this dream to explore feelings of losing connection or facing life alone.
- If you are abandoning others and feel liberated in your dream, this may be a prompt to leave people or situations that no longer serve you.

# Baptism

This prophetic dream has profound implications. It can symbolize a rite of passage, rebirth, deep awakening, connection with the higher self, spiritual renewal and personal transformation.

It can also represent a cleansing of old attitudes, a deep connection with one's faith, an opening to the deep unconscious, new possibilities and healing.

For some, it can indicate the ritual leaving of the self-centred life for a life of service.

## Interpretations

- Baptism by water can relate to emotions, community and fellowship, as well as a change of heart, or a desire to have one's longings quenched.
- Baptism by fire suggests a powerful cleansing and burning away of the old self.
- Baptism by blood or wine can reflect a link you are making with society and humanity.
- Baptism by sound or energy can refer to an immersion with the cosmos.

## Opportunities for growth

- Use this dream to consider how you are living your life and whether you are ready for deep spiritual changes.
- This dream can inspire you to become more involved with your community by offering service and help in some way.

# Celebrities

Celebrities showing up in your dreams – from actors and musicians to athletes and politicians – are archetypal symbols of luxury, lifestyle, health and empowerment. They are all about rising to the top and self-expression.

A friend who becomes famous in a dream reflects your fears they will find someone better.

## Interpretations

- Dreaming of celebrities could show that you are seeking inspiration or aspiring to be successful.
- This dream could also represent a wish to be taken seriously or point to underlying issues to do with self-esteem.
- A celebrity in your dream could reveal a desire to gain popularity within your environment.
- A celebrity hook-up could show a boredom within your current relationship.

## Opportunities for growth

- Dreaming about becoming a celebrity is a positive sign that you are ready to be your authentic self.
- Use this dream to plough on with any aspirations or long-term life goals.

# Children

If you are having dreams of children, this can represent a link to your inner child, and those elements of playfulness, innocence, joy and wonder we can often lose touch with as adults.

There are many variations of this dream, with just as many interpretations.

Sometimes, dreaming of children can indicate new relationships or moving on to another stage of maturity. These types of dreams can also reveal the need to nurture yourself as you would have liked as a child.

## Interpretations

- If you dream of giving birth to a child, this could mark some acceptance of a major life change.
- If you dream of becoming a child, you yearn for a more playful way of being.
- If you dream of being stuck in a child's body, you may be stuck in a fantasy world.
- A happy, healthy child in your dream means positive changes are afoot.
- If you dream of a caged child, it reveals a need to reconnect with your sense of joy and wonder.

## Opportunities for growth

- Use this type of dream to reflect on your current feelings of dependency and vulnerability.
- Dreaming about unhappy children or being an unhappy child is a sign to make more room for spontaneity, harmony, joy and play.

# Choir

Harmony, co-operation, teamwork, unity and collaboration are all possible themes in this uplifting dream.

Dreaming of a choir can represent those with common goals and similar beliefs putting their individual efforts together to achieve a higher purpose.

This dream can reveal feelings of pleasure, happiness and love, bound up in this act of joyful celebration.

Dreams involving a choir can symbolize being in touch with your emotions, and having the ability to express them. It can also link to a sense of belonging, connection and community, as well as success and accomplishment.

## Interpretations

- Hearing a beautiful voice in uplifting song in your dream can suggest good news.
- Hearing others singing is a sign that support is coming.
- Dreams of a church choir can represent a longing for spirituality and guidance.
- An out-of-tune choir suggests possible misunderstandings with family.
- If there is one person singing out of tune in your dream, check your business dealings.
- Performing with a choir means you are growing spiritually and accepting yourself.

## Opportunities for growth

- If your dream features joyous singing in a choir, take advantage of this good omen and look for opportunities that may arise.
- If your dream features a less tuneful choir or singer, be alert to any disharmony or disagreement in your work or home life.

# Divorce or relationship disharmony

Dreaming about divorce, whether it involves yourself or someone close to you, can be upsetting, but it is important to remember that, particularly in this case, dreams are a tool to explore the psyche and are not a foreshadowing of things to come.

After such a dream, try to reflect on your current circumstances – it may be about confronting a fear of losing your partner, or reveal a fear of staying single.

It can also be unrelated to romantic relationships, and be more about the need to separate yourself from a job, situation or person that no longer serves your growth.

## Interpretations

- If you dream of parents or close friends getting divorced, this can reflect anxieties around losing support.
- If you dream that your spouse wants a divorce, it could mean signifying a new phase in your life.
- If you tell your spouse you want a divorce in your dream, you are trying to let go.
- If you are pregnant and getting divorced in your dream, this could reveal new directions and a period of change, growth and creativity.
- If a partner appears to be hiding something in your dream, this could reveal your own feelings of guilt within the relationship.

## Opportunities for growth

- Take time to reflect on whether you are going through a period of change, or even a new phase in your life.
- Seek out what you can look forward to in this transition.

# Engagement

A dream of engagement can vary in meaning. Most often, it promises a formalizing of relationships and important decisions. It can also point to a deep need to feel desirable and wanted.

In some instances, it can symbolize a commitment that will take some working through, with a desire to improve a situation, romantically or professionally.

A key theme of this dream is staying committed to your aspirations and goals.

## Interpretations

- Seeing yourself engaged means you are about to make a deeper commitment.
- If an engagement ring is on the left hand, a new project or opportunity offers growth.
- If an engagement ring is on the right hand, your ex or your past still grips you.
- Losing an engagement ring means change is heading your way.
- If you become engaged to a stranger, it can symbolize a lack of emotional support or anxiety around making a rash decision.

## Opportunities for growth

- This dream offers a chance to look at what you could work harder at to get to where you need to be.
- It can serve as an opportunity to improve a relationship with a loved one.

# Infidelity

A partner cheating on you in a dream can be a signal of betrayal, insecurity or miscommunication. It can also offer a signpost toward unaddressed issues in the relationship.

While these dreams can symbolize emotional dissatisfaction, sexual frustration or unresolved emotions around past infidelities, they can also be an indication of anxieties, fears and unmet needs within a present partnership.

## Interpretations

- If you dream about your partner cheating with a stranger, it can mean you are missing quality time with them.
- If your partner cheats with their ex, there is some jealousy around the qualities of the ex in question.
- If you cheat on your pregnant partner, this reflects a common fear that your partner now has a more important relationship than the one with you.

## Opportunities for growth

- If your partner cheats with someone you know in your dream, look at your insecurities around other people in your life, and whether you need to boost your self-worth, or need more reassurance from your partner.
- If you have a dream that you are "caught in the act", ask yourself: what are you feeling guilt about?

# Deceased loved ones

These dreams can be very commonplace, but they remain a special experience, and one markedly different from a normal dream. In fact, these dreams are reported as being among the most vivid, memorable and clear, and tend to be quite positive.

Researchers state the most common contact with the deceased occurs in the dream state. It can be seen as a normal part of healing, a way of grieving or a processing of repressed feelings. It is often considered to be like a hand reaching out through the doorway of the spirits, frequently leaving the dreamer with a profound feeling of peace.

These dreams can involve children lost during pregnancies, parents who passed away when their children were young, pets, partners and various family members.

## Interpretations

- If you dream of a specific loved one who is deceased, it points not only to grieving but to processing, and accepting, that loss.

- Sometimes when dreaming of a deceased loved one, you can feel as if you are receiving information or reassurance about their passing, and it can even represent a communication with the soul that has passed over.

- Dreaming of loved ones who have passed may also mean that you are dealing with stress or unresolved issues unrelated to them. These dreams use feelings of grief to make you aware of what is not yet resolved.

## Opportunities for growth

- These types of dreams can often bring a sense of peace and closure to your relationship with that special person.

- Take time to remember a loved one during the day, sharing the dream you had with others and swapping memories.

# Chapter Four

## NATURE

Animals

Earth

Fire

Food

Gardens

Horizon

Ice

Lightning

Mountains

Water

# Animals

Dreams involving animals are often associated with the recovery of wholeness and an intuitiveness about the natural world.

It can show dormant, powerful energies rising into your conscious mind, guiding you away from the part of the self that is critical and conformist.

If your dream contains wild animals, this can point toward a need to reconnect to our uncivilized, instinctive and primal selves.

If you dream of beasts of burden (a plough horse or herding dog, for example), this can suggest you are feeling yoked to a heavy responsibility.

## Interpretations

- Dogs represent loyalty and companionship.
- Cats represent intuition and independence as well as trusting your instincts.
- Birds suggest freedom and inspiration as well as a need to nurture your ambition and vision.
- Snakes can mean there will be a transformation, a shedding of skin or a rebirth in your life.
- Horses reflect finding strength and having the freedom to pursue your dreams.
- Spiders represent patience and creativity as well as a will to create your desired life.
- Lions symbolize courage and leadership.

## Opportunities for growth

- If you dream of a domestic animal such as a pet, work on cherishing your present relationships.
- Dreaming about birds or cats may inspire you to be freer and more instinctual.

# Earth

Having a dream regarding Earth itself can often be associated with stability, stillness and grounding.

This type of dream will be allied to your foundation and your belief systems, and can be quite symbolic of a powerful unconscious feminine energy.

Dreaming of Earth can also represent growth and balance within your environment. How Earth appears in your dream reflects the balance of your inner world.

## Interpretations

- Dreams of Earth falling reflects emotions out of their correct orbit.
- If the ground opens up in your dream, the image is linked to your own unconscious "opening".
- Uneven ground shows a path that must be navigated carefully.
- Dreams of rocky ground means that it can be difficult to make projects bloom where you are.
- Dreams of muddy ground indicates you may be undertaking a transformation.
- Solid ground can represent a good foundation for future ventures.

## Opportunities for growth

- Dreams of the entire Earth can offer a chance to reflect on your life and take conscious steps toward making it better.
- If dreaming of unstable ground, look closely at how you can get through what might be difficult situation.

# Fire

This ancient symbol is used for ceremonies marking transformation and initiation, and in dreams is heavily associated with rites of passage.

Many fire dreams focus on themes of purification, illumination, passion, transformation and warmth.

Notice the objects in your dream fire and whether people are present or not. This can help you understand more fully if these themes are general or associated with a particular person.

## Interpretations

- Fire dreams can mean motivation – for a project, idea or vision. Starting a fire can symbolize the creation of an idea or venture.
- Alternatively, a fire dream can represent an uncontrolled rage or slow-burning anger, or even reflect intense feelings of longing and love.
- If someone is trying to put the fire out, look at people in your life who extinguish your energy.
- A dream of being on fire can signify new beginnings.

## Opportunities for growth

- Watching something burn and then reflecting on that feeling you had can be a cathartic experience.
- If people are present in your fire dream, try to intuit what they mean to you from the meanings above.

# Food

Dream food can be received, offered, cooked, bought, spilt, shared or burnt. And while not unusual, dreams of food can carry a multitude of meanings.

Occasions surrounding food can also hold significance in dreams, from banquets to special holiday meals.

Too much or not enough food can also reveal difficulties in other areas of your life.

## Interpretations

- Feasts or banquets can reveal a personal accomplishment, such as the end of an emotional challenge. They may also show longing for community.
- Sweet foods relate to craving pleasure and carefree moments.
- Bitter foods can reflect difficult moments that must be faced.
- Bread points to our experiences with the divine.
- Ample food symbolizes a time of plenty, enjoyment and sensual pleasures.
- Bad food represents something toxic or unpalatable you are "ingesting". It could be a belief, relationship, media or behaviour.

## Opportunities for growth

- If you are unable to eat food in your dream, look for situations where you are starved of support.
- If you are eating badly in your dream, try to unearth what in life is not working for you.

# Gardens

A garden is a place of conscious order, renewal and rejuvenation. It is a sacred space allowing growth of the inner self.

This dream asks us to slow down and enjoy life. It points to a need for relaxation, and a desire to reconnect with nature.

Feelings of awe, peace, purity, escape and wonder are bound up in a dream involving gardens. Ideas of creation, innocence, femininity and fertility are central to this symbol.

## Interpretations

- A beautiful garden means wealth can grow.
- A highly manicured garden represents organized, but also rigid, individuals.
- A garden containing a variety of fruit, vegetables and flowers shows positive change is approaching.
- A vegetable garden indicates productive times ahead.
- If the garden is overgrown, pay attention to your relationships and self-care.
- Fruit trees in bloom mean marriage or pleasure.

## Opportunities for growth

- Revel in the positive feelings of dreaming about gardens, using that sense of rejuvenation to bloom even further.
- If your dream garden is too overgrown or sprawling, look to improving your care and attention to yourself and others.

# Horizon

The symbol of the horizon has multiple interpretations, depending upon the context of the dream.

As the meeting place of the earth and sky, it is traditionally associated with boundaries and possibilities, but is also seen as a place of hope and promise.

In dreams, it often presents as a threshold between the known and the unknown. It can become a place of illumination, infinite potential and new beginnings, and can even represent a journey's end.

## Interpretations

- Dreaming of the horizon may represent a goal, the desire for adventure, a moment of closure or major transitions and life changes.
- A clear vibrant horizon signifies hope and confidence.
- A partially obscured, hazy or out-of-focus horizon represents challenges and the need for clarity.
- A morning horizon can be linked to new beginnings.
- An evening horizon can represent a conclusion you are unprepared for.

## Opportunities for growth

- Use this dream to broaden your perspectives.
- You may need to get uncomfortable before you can realize personal growth.

# Ice

Dreams of ice can encourage you to journey into difficult and unexplored territory, often wrestling with trapped feelings, frozen emotions, coldness, rigidity or indifference.

If there are traumas making you feel stuck, blocked, paralyzed or cut off from life, these will need to be processed and released.

As you give these areas the attention they need, you will thaw out, soften and open to a more balanced and joyful state.

## Interpretations

- Road ice represents challenging conditions with a message of perseverance.
- Melting ice is a positive sign of releasing emotions.
- Icebergs can motivate you to seek out the unexplored parts within yourself.
- Clear ice speaks to ideas of purity and clarity.
- Walking on ice signals caution and reflection.

## Opportunities for growth

- Ice encourages you to show your natural feelings and return to the flow of life.
- Consider how to bring more warmth into your life – perhaps through joy, laughter and connection.

# Lightning

This complex dream symbol from the heavens is linked to clarity, moments of searing illumination, immeasurable energy, powerful visual displays, motivation, fertility, the destruction of ignorance and divine intervention.

It can also be a metaphoric symbol of a "eureka" moment, foretelling a clearer comprehension of a situation.

It can even symbolize repressed feelings that threaten a situation with destruction if released.

## Interpretations

- Lightning can shock the dreamer out of a rut.
- It can be a premonition of sudden and unexpected change.
- Dreaming of being struck by lightning is a cosmic wake-up call.
- Lightning dreams can be a warning of danger.
- The louder the thunder that accompanies the lightning, the more important the dream.

## Opportunities for growth

- Use these types of shocking dreams to wake yourself up, metaphorically, and take action.

# Mountains

In our waking life, mountains can evoke feelings of humbleness, wonder and awe.

In dreams, they are a metaphor for aspiring consciousness and our inner journeys, representing major obstacles and challenges. They can also symbolize firmness, eternity and stillness.

Mountain dreams are associated with good luck, growth and the search for clarity. They can represent challenges to be worked through in work, finance, relationships or health.

## Interpretations

- Dreaming of being on top of the mountain means that you are realizing your goals.
- Climbing a mountain has links to perseverance, passion and determination.
- Facing a mountain means you are faced with an unavoidable situation.
- Dreams of green mountains represent wealth and success.
- Dreaming of coming down a mountain symbolizes relief.
- Dreaming of mountains can represent your own high expectations or a tendency to overdramatize.

## Opportunities for growth

- Use this dream to work through challenges in your life without giving up on your goals.
- Embrace the steadfast symbolism that a mountain offers, bringing comfort if you are experiencing a lot of change.

# Water

Water is often a window into our subconscious states, in both dream and waking life.

Water can symbolize life, death, change, rebirth, renewal, cleanliness, purity and the unconscious, so remembering the context and feelings that surround your specific water dream is important.

Water is linked to the emotions of your waking life, whether they are calm or erratic, measured or chaotic.

## Interpretations

- Dreaming of a tidal wave represents change.
- Drowning dreams symbolize feeling overwhelmed by emotions and can be a way of processing challenging situations.
- Dreaming of a strong river current that bashes you around shows a life out of control.
- Swimming pool dreams, if alone, can reflect feelings of being trapped. If someone is in a pool with you, it shows a deep connection.
- Being underwater in your dream relates to inescapable stress and overwhelming emotions.
- Murky water symbolizes feelings of doubt and insecurity; clear water shows clarity.

## Opportunities for growth

- The state of the ocean reflects your emotional state - notice calm waters, heavy currents or strong tides.
- Turbulent water is a sign to take time to slow down and reflect on ways to manage stress.

# Chapter Five

## OBJECTS & ITEMS

# Colours

The colours of clothes and objects may hold meaning within a dream. Noticing colours in dreams can provide an emotional framework and give an additional layer of meaning when viewed alongside other symbolism.

If one colour is clear and ascendant, it can be linked to a dominant emotional state.

Generally, light, vibrant or pastel colours are connected with safety, hope and happiness.

Very dark shades often represent emotional states of fear, anxiety or even terror.

Of course, this can vary with the individual. Colours can have different meanings between cultures, or hold specific memories for dreamers.

## Interpretations

- Red represents anger, desire, sexuality, passion, confidence and excitement.
- Orange can mean change, warmth, vitality and endurance.
- Blue shows clarity, openness, sadness, masculinity, truth and seriousness.
- Green represents growth, fertility, envy, healing and peace.
- White can mean innocence, spirituality, faith and medicine.
- Black can symbolize grief, night, anarchy, formality and the unknown.

## Opportunities for growth

- Use the colours and objects in your dream to focus on what each means to you personally, then adapt the above interpretations to suit.

# Gold

This rare and valuable metal is an ancient symbol, long associated with things we treasure.

It encompasses feelings of wealth, power, success, eternity, reward, good luck and riches, but also carries ideas of royalty and prestige.

In dreams, it can be linked to ideas of fulfilment and happiness.

## Interpretations

- Dreams of gold bars or coins point to finding something within you of great value.
- Losing gold is not necessarily money related – it can be a warning about losing something valuable.
- Receiving gold is a symbol of being gifted something valuable.
- Seeing the colour gold can symbolize those things you value most in life.

## Opportunities for growth

- Take advantage of this illustrious dream to embrace new opportunities.
- Let joy into your life and enrich your future.

# Hooks

Dreams with hooks in them can be positive or negative depending upon the situation they are found in and the actions taken with them.

Most typically, a hook in a dream can represent determination and hope. It can also be a sign of encouragement.

A hook, especially if it is giving you negative feelings in the dream, can also signify a trap or addiction, or indicate you are being caught in some kind of mischief or deceit.

## Interpretations

- Dreaming of finding a hook is a signal of positive change.
- Catching fish with a hook signifies being in charge of your life.
- Being caught on a hook may mean you are feeling trapped and controlled by someone or something else.
- Breaking a hook can symbolize ending a situation you feel has control over you.

## Opportunities for growth

- If accompanied by positive feelings, use this dream to persevere and go after the things you have always wanted.
- If you are attached to the hook, try to work out what got you there, and what you can do about it.

# Knives

Knives tend to bring up feelings of danger, harm or fear in our waking lives. But a knife dream can also represent the removal of something, a fear of being hurt, or a personally confronting insight.

A dream involving knives can bring up themes of separation, sharpness, danger, confrontation and destruction, along with feelings of anxiety, fear, unease and vulnerability.

This dream advises you to approach elements of your life with caution. It asks which parts are out of control or negative.

## Interpretations

- Fighting with knives represents anxiety and survival.
- A stab wound shows you are harbouring unresolved emotional pain.
- Dreams of cutting can mean the severing of entanglements or obstacles.
- Holding a knife signifies moving away from a relationship.

## Opportunities for growth

- To fully understand a knife dream's meaning, you must fully explore the emotions and context within it before rushing to interpretation.
- Review your knife dream carefully, possibly removing things in your life that are no longer serving you.

# Letters

Letters – receiving them, sending them, reading them – can be revealing and exciting in a dream.

They may represent a new understanding, something unexpected or a realization.

They can also be seen as a symbol of self-knowledge or of new opportunities, or could foretell a situation that comes with a potential for self-awareness.

## Interpretations

- A love letter is a sign you have completed a task or that you are closing a life chapter.
- If a postal worker delivers the letter, it signifies you will receive something unexpectedly.
- Sealing a letter is a sign that there are secrets in your life.
- Tearing a letter implies annoyances ahead.
- Receiving a letter from an ex shows a desire to reconnect.
- The more attractive the paper, handwriting and stamp is on the letter, the better the news!

## Opportunities for growth

- Focus on anything that has been puzzling you – perhaps an understanding, or a new piece of the puzzle, is not far away.

# Mirrors

Mirrors in dreams are a potent message. They often reflect the dreamer's image, feelings and actions right back at them, urging them to focus on introspection and self-awareness.

Common themes in mirror dreams can include reversal, observation, vanity, the truth of the matter, luck, illusion and vulnerabilities.

The image found within the mirror can carry the possibility of profound change, where flawed behaviours become unrecognizable to the new you. Seeing a mirror in a dream can prompt you to explore hidden aspects of yourself in the journey toward an authentic you.

## Interpretations

- A dream containing a distorted circus-mirror vision of yourself highlights fears and hidden insecurities.
- Looking into a mirror and seeing yourself is an acknowledgement of your strengths.
- Looking into a mirror and seeing someone else symbolizes feelings of inauthenticity.
- A dream with a broken mirror is a call to let go of illusions and reach for significant change.

## Opportunities for growth

- Dream mirrors are a call for introspection and self-awareness.
- Be sure to take a good look at what your subconscious is trying to tell you!

# Musical instruments

In both the waking and the dream world, musical instruments can stimulate emotions of reverence and joy, expressing the flow of life.

Dreams could involve playing an instrument or listening to evocative music.

Dreams involving musical instruments are particularly linked to a call to become more self-aware. They can also reveal an awakening of creative impulses.

## Interpretations

- Hearing music points to a spiritual significance.
- Dreaming of performing music represents a desire to grow to your potential.
- Dreams that involve playing a musical instrument in time show you are on your correct path.
- Playing large complex instruments relates to the mind and intellect.
- Playing percussion instruments links to the rhythm of life.
- Dreaming of soft, soothing sounds can mean good news, while loud, disturbing sounds can relate to the disclosure of hidden things.

## Opportunities for growth

- If one or two notes only are being played, try to move yourself into a fuller range of emotions.
- Embrace your creative side (not only musically), and explore new hobbies.

# Numbers

Numbers in dreamscapes offer glimpses into the deeper psyche. They are traditionally associated with organization and order, symbolizing the search for logic and understanding.

Numbers may also symbolize specific people or events. They may also be reminders of special occasions.

Numbers can have various meanings linking to the dreamer's personal associations and their culture.

# Interpretations

**1** Indicates new beginnings, individuality, fresh chapters and taking initiative.

**2** Focuses on dualities, partnership, connection and teamwork.

**3** Represents progress, creativity and personal growth.

**4** Indicates stability, security and practicality.

**5** Speaks to positive changes, trust and transformation.

**6** Is associated with healing, harmony and self-care.

**7** Symbolizes intuition, spiritual understanding and self-reflection.

**8** Reveals material success, perseverance and financial stability.

**9** Represents completions, closure or the ending of a chapter.

**10** Is associated with potential, a blank canvas and divinity.

**11** Repeating numbers point to things lining up.

# Pyramids

Themes of mystery, great achievements, the search for spirituality and timelessness are bound up in this awe-inspiring symbol.

This powerful shape can signify a transformation, show a longing for esoteric knowledge, or simply represent feelings of stability.

If you are searching for treasure within a pyramid, your dream may be about discovering your own hidden talents.

## Interpretations

- Dreaming of a pyramid with the capstone missing symbolizes frustrations about feeling unable to reach your potential.
- Climbing a pyramid represents your growth or progression toward your goals.
- If you dream of standing on top of a pyramid, this can show accomplishment and mastery.
- A dream of being inside a pyramid means making time for introspection and intuition.

## Opportunities for growth

- Use this potent symbol to seek and discover the mysteries within yourself, nurturing the talent and knowledge hiding in plain sight.

**“Dreams are today’s answers to tomorrow’s questions.”**

Edgar Cayce,
*On Dreams* (1968)